in a
WORLD
where You can
BE
anything . . .

blue sparrow

Design by Ashley Wirfel

ISBN: 978-1-63582-092-8 (hardcover)

10   9   8   7   6   5   4   3   2   1

Printed in the United States of America

FIRST EDITION

in a
WORLD
where you can
BE
anything . . .

MATTHEW KELLY

BLUE SPARROW BOOKS
North Palm Beach, Florida

INTRODUCTION

We live in a world of unlimited possibilities, but too often we get caught up in the day-to-day realities of life and the hustle and bustle of the world and lose sight of all that is possible.

The busier our lives become, the more important it is to live with great intentionality. The more options we have before us, the more important it is to discern and decide with great intentionality. And living with great intentionality requires that we step back from time to time and think about life. We live more fulfilling lives when we pause each day to think about who we are, what we are here for, what matters most, what matters least, and our hopes and dreams for tomorrow.

We all have good qualities, we all have qualities we want to eradicate, and we all have qualities we aspire to. What's your best quality? What are your top ten qualities? What qualities do you aspire to? What qualities do you most admire in other people? What qualities do you look for in a friend? What qualities do you look for in a lover?

In A World Where You Can Be Anything . . . is designed to get you thinking about who you are, who you want to be, and who you are capable of being. I hope it opens new possibilities for you in every area of your life.

As human beings we are continually invited to explore new horizons. Let's not allow the hustle and bustle of this world to distract us. Let's not get so busy with all the things that will mean nothing to nobody a year or two from now that we lose ourselves.

I overheard someone say the other day, "If it won't matter five years from now, it doesn't matter." It made me smile. I have always been attracted to this kind of practical wisdom.

You are here to become the-very-best-version-of-yourself. Try not to lose sight of that. It is a very powerful idea. The idea of becoming the-best-version-of-yourself brings light and clarity to every situation in our lives, empowering us to make great decisions one moment at a time.

Every day in every way you are becoming a-better-version-of-yourself. Is this true? Maybe it is and maybe it isn't, but that is all in the past now. Starting today, beginning right now, in each moment, choose the-best-version-of-yourself.

We are people of possibility. Most possibilities are unseen and unexplored, but it's time to change that. In a world where you can be anything . . . be . . .

IN A **WORLD** WHERE YOU CAN **BE** **ANYTHING . . .**

be yourself!

In a world where
YOU CAN
be anything . . .

BE GENEROUS!

In a world
where you can
be anything . . .

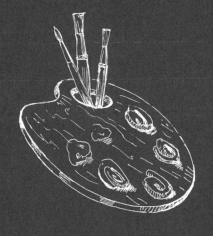

be creative!

In a world where
YOU CAN
be anything . . .

BE CURIOUS!

IN A **WORLD**
WHERE
YOU CAN
BE
ANYTHING . . .

be kind!

In a world where
YOU CAN
be anything . . .

BE SPONTANEOUS!

In a world
where you can
be anything . . .

be healthy!

In a world where
YOU CAN
be anything . . .

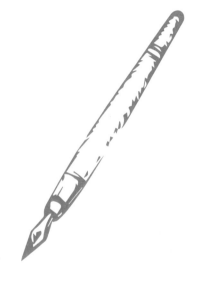

BE THOUGHTFUL!

IN A **WORLD** WHERE YOU CAN **BE** **ANYTHING ...**

be romantic!

In a world where
YOU CAN
be anything . . .

BE OPEN!

IN A **WORLD**
WHERE
YOU CAN
BE
ANYTHING . . .

be disciplined!

In a world where
YOU CAN
be anything . . .

BE A READER!

IN A **WORLD**
WHERE
YOU CAN
BE
ANYTHING . . .

be a dreamer!

In a world where
YOU CAN
be anything . . .

BE A LOVER!

IN A **WORLD**
WHERE
YOU CAN
BE
ANYTHING . . .

be courageous!

In a world where
YOU CAN
be anything . . .

BE RESPECTFUL!

IN A **WORLD**
WHERE
YOU CAN
BE
ANYTHING . . .

be amazing!

In a world where
YOU CAN
be anything . . .

BE HONEST!

In a world
where you can
be anything . . .

be adventurous!

IN A **WORLD**
WHERE
YOU CAN
BE
ANYTHING . . .

be funny!

IN A **WORLD**
WHERE
YOU CAN
BE
ANYTHING . . .

be compassionate!

In a world where

YOU CAN

be anything . . .

BE INTRIGUING!

In a world
where you can
be anything . . .

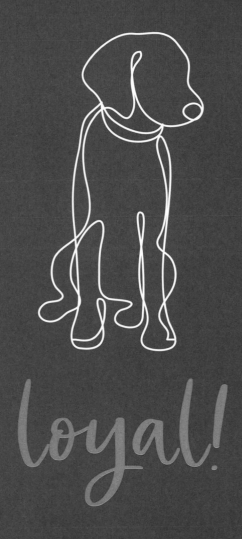

be loyal!

In a world where
YOU CAN
be anything . . .

BE FORGIVING!

IN A **WORLD**
WHERE
YOU CAN
BE
ANYTHING . . .

be excellent!

In a world where
YOU CAN
be anything . . .

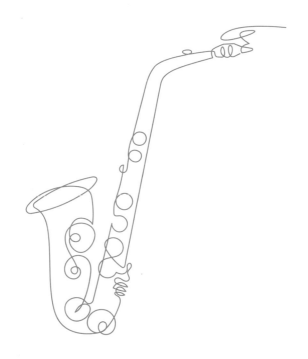

BE SOULFUL!

IN A **WORLD**
WHERE
YOU CAN
BE
ANYTHING . . .

be authentic!

IN A **WORLD**
WHERE
YOU CAN
BE
ANYTHING . . .

be grateful!

In a world where
YOU CAN
be anything...

BE PATIENT!

IN A **WORLD** WHERE YOU CAN **BE ANYTHING** . . .

be tenacious!

IN A **WORLD**
WHERE
YOU CAN
BE
ANYTHING . . .

be empathetic!

In a world where
YOU CAN
be anything . . .

BE PERSISTENT!

IN A **WORLD**
WHERE
YOU CAN
BE
ANYTHING . . .

be assertive!

In a world where
YOU CAN
be anything . . .

BE A CONTINUOUS LEARNER!

IN A **WORLD**
WHERE
YOU CAN
BE
ANYTHING . . .

be adaptable!

IN A **WORLD**
WHERE
YOU CAN
BE
ANYTHING . . .

be hopeful!

In a world where
YOU CAN
be anything . . .

BE ATTENTIVE!

In a world where
YOU CAN
be anything . . .

BE GENTLE!

IN A **WORLD**
WHERE
YOU CAN
BE
ANYTHING . . .

be charitable!

In a world where
YOU CAN
be anything . . .

BE MERCIFUL!

IN A **WORLD** WHERE YOU CAN **BE** **ANYTHING . . .**

be enthusiastic!

In a world
where you can
be anything . . .

be peaceful!

In a world where
YOU CAN
be anything . . .

BE HUMBLE!

In a world where
YOU CAN
be anything . . .

BE TRUSTWORTHY!

IN A **WORLD**
WHERE
YOU CAN
BE
ANYTHING . . .

be bold!

IN A **WORLD**
WHERE
YOU CAN
BE
ANYTHING . . .

be joyful!

In a world where
YOU CAN
be anything . . .

BE SINCERE!

In a world where
YOU CAN
be anything . . .

BE JUST!

IN A **WORLD**
WHERE
YOU CAN
BE
ANYTHING . . .

be friendly!

In a world where
YOU CAN
be anything . . .

BE STILL!

In a world
where you can
be anything . . .

be wise!

IN A **WORLD** WHERE YOU CAN **BE** **ANYTHING** . . .

be spiritual!

In a world where
YOU CAN
be anything . . .

BE ALL YOU CAN BE!

IN A **WORLD** WHERE YOU CAN **BE ANYTHING . . .**

be optimistic!

IN A **WORLD**
WHERE
YOU CAN
BE
ANYTHING . . .

be confident!

In a world where
YOU CAN
be anything . . .

BE FUN!

IN A **WORLD**
WHERE
YOU CAN
BE
ANYTHING . . .

be hardworking!

In a world where
YOU CAN
be anything . . .

BE RESOURCEFUL!

In a world
where you can
be anything . . .

be a thinker!

IN A **WORLD**
WHERE
YOU CAN
BE
ANYTHING . . .

be sensitive!

In a world where
YOU CAN
be anything . . .

BE EDUCATED!

In a world where
YOU CAN
be anything . . .

BE UNDERSTANDING!

IN A **WORLD**
WHERE
YOU CAN
BE
ANYTHING . . .

be independent!

In a world
where you can
be anything . . .

be musical!

In a world where

YOU CAN

be anything . . .

BE TOLERANT!

IN A **WORLD**
WHERE
YOU CAN
BE
ANYTHING . . .

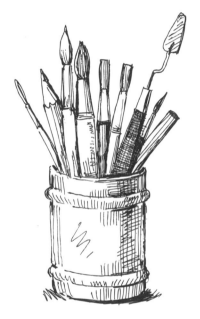

be artistic!

IN A **WORLD** WHERE YOU CAN **BE** **ANYTHING . . .**

be perfectly
imperfect!

In a world where
YOU CAN
be anything . . .

BE CHARMING!

IN A **WORLD**
WHERE
YOU CAN
BE
ANYTHING . . .

be logical!

In a world where
YOU CAN
be anything . . .

BE AWESOME!

In a world where
YOU CAN
be anything...

BE LOW-MAINTENANCE!

IN A **WORLD** WHERE YOU CAN **BE** **ANYTHING . . .**

be athletic!

IN A **WORLD**
WHERE
YOU CAN
BE
ANYTHING . . .

be inspirational!

In a world where
YOU CAN
be anything . . .

BE GOOD
WITH MONEY!

IN A **WORLD**
WHERE
YOU CAN
BE
ANYTHING . . .

be an influencer!

IN A **WORLD**
WHERE
YOU CAN
BE
ANYTHING . . .

be happy!

IN A **WORLD**
WHERE
YOU CAN
BE
ANYTHING . . .

be passionate!

In a world where
YOU CAN
be anything . . .

BE FREE!

IN A **WORLD**
WHERE
YOU CAN
BE
ANYTHING . . .

be intimate!

In a world where
YOU CAN
be anything . . .

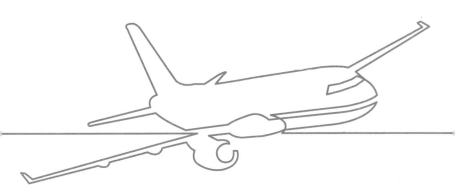

BE A TRAVELER!

In a world where
YOU CAN
be anything . . .

BE WILD!

IN A **WORLD** WHERE YOU CAN **BE** **ANYTHING . . .**

be a leader!

IN A **WORLD**
WHERE
YOU CAN
BE
ANYTHING . . .

be a good son,
daughter, brother,
sister, mother,
father!

In a world where
YOU CAN
be anything . . .

BE ONE WITH GOD!

IN A **WORLD**
WHERE
YOU CAN
BE
ANYTHING . . .

be a problem
solver!

In a world where
YOU CAN
be anything . . .

BE AMBITIOUS!

IN A **WORLD**
WHERE
YOU CAN
BE
ANYTHING . . .

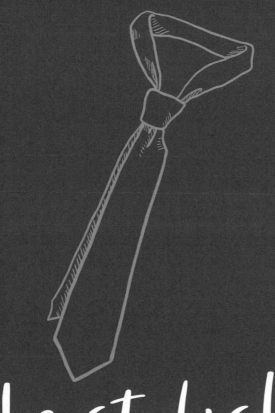

be stylish!

IN A **WORLD**
WHERE
YOU CAN
BE
ANYTHING . . .

be in love
with life!

In a world where
YOU CAN
be anything...

BE CLASSY!

In a world where
YOU CAN
be anything . . .

BE A REASON
TO BELIEVE!

IN A **WORLD**
WHERE
YOU CAN
BE
ANYTHING . . .

be different!

In a world where
YOU CAN
be anything . . .

BE AN ENCOURAGER!

IN A **WORLD**
WHERE
YOU CAN
BE
ANYTHING . . .

be intuitive!

IN A **WORLD**
WHERE
YOU CAN
BE
ANYTHING . . .

be dynamic!

In a world where
YOU CAN
be anything . . .

BE A GREAT DECISION MAKER!

In a world where

YOU CAN

be anything . . .

BE THOUGHT PROVOKING!

IN A **WORLD** WHERE YOU CAN **BE** **ANYTHING** . . .

be dependable!

In a world where
YOU CAN
be anything . . .

BE WARM!

IN A **WORLD**
WHERE
YOU CAN
BE
ANYTHING . . .

be kindhearted!

In a world where
YOU CAN
be anything . . .

BE UNSELFISH!

In a world where
YOU CAN
be anything . . .

BE OPEN-MINDED!

IN A **WORLD**
WHERE
YOU CAN
BE
ANYTHING . . .

be lovable!

IN A **WORLD** WHERE YOU CAN **BE** **ANYTHING** . . .

be appreciative!

In a world where
YOU CAN
be anything . . .

BE ORIGINAL!

IN A **WORLD** WHERE YOU CAN **BE** **ANYTHING . . .**

be conscientious!

In a world where
YOU CAN
be anything . . .

BE ETHICAL!

In a world
where you can
be anything . . .

be observant!

IN A **WORLD**
WHERE
YOU CAN
BE
ANYTHING . . .

be sensible!

In a world where
YOU CAN
be anything . . .

BE ENERGETIC!

In a world where
YOU CAN
be anything . . .

BE SYMPATHETIC!

IN A **WORLD**
WHERE
YOU CAN
BE
ANYTHING . . .

be tender!

IN A **WORLD**
WHERE
YOU CAN
BE
ANYTHING . . .

be a light!

In a world where
YOU CAN
be anything . . .

BE CULTURED!

In a world where
YOU CAN
be anything . . .

BE REALISTIC & UNREALISTIC!

IN A **WORLD** WHERE YOU CAN **BE ANYTHING . . .**

be relaxed!

In a world where
YOU CAN
be anything . . .

BE DIGNIFIED!

In a world where
YOU CAN
be anything . . .

BE A WARRIOR!

IN A **WORLD**
WHERE
YOU CAN
BE
ANYTHING . . .

be happy for others when good things happen!

IN A **WORLD**
WHERE
YOU CAN
BE
ANYTHING . . .

be childlike!

In a world where
YOU CAN
be anything . . .

BE OPEN TO CHANGE!

IN A **WORLD**
WHERE
YOU CAN
BE
ANYTHING . . .

be accepting!

In a world where
YOU CAN
be anything . . .

BE EXTRAVAGANT!

IN A **WORLD**
WHERE
YOU CAN
BE
ANYTHING . . .

be graceful!

In a world where
YOU CAN
be anything . . .

BE SILLY!

IN A **WORLD**
WHERE
YOU CAN
BE
ANYTHING . . .

be worry-free!

In a world
where you can
be anything . . .

be punctual!

In a world where
YOU CAN
be anything . . .

BE MINDFUL OF OTHER PEOPLE'S NEEDS!

IN A **WORLD**
WHERE
YOU CAN
BE
ANYTHING . . .

be a lover
of nature!

IN A **WORLD**
WHERE
YOU CAN
BE
ANYTHING . . .

be helpful!

In a world where
YOU CAN
be anything . . .

BE BRILLIANT!

IN A **WORLD** WHERE YOU CAN **BE ANYTHING** . . .

be interesting!

In a world where
YOU CAN
be anything . . .

BE ALTRUISTIC!

IN A **WORLD**
WHERE
YOU CAN
BE
ANYTHING . . .

be cheerful!

In a world where
YOU CAN
be anything . . .

BE IMAGINATIVE!

In a world where

YOU CAN

be anything . . .

BE FLEXIBLE!

IN A **WORLD** WHERE YOU CAN **BE ANYTHING** . . .

be diplomatic!

IN A **WORLD** WHERE YOU CAN **BE** **ANYTHING . . .**

be positive!

In a world where
YOU CAN
be anything . . .

BE A GOOD
LISTENER!

IN A **WORLD** WHERE YOU CAN **BE ANYTHING** . . .

be prepared!

In a world where
YOU CAN
be anything . . .

BE RELIABLE!

IN A **WORLD**
WHERE
YOU CAN
BE
ANYTHING . . .

be a lover of
little things!

In a world where
YOU CAN
be anything...

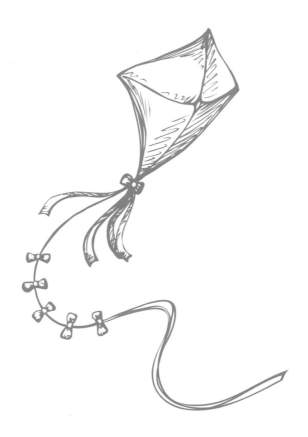

BE UPLIFTING!

In a world where
YOU CAN
be anything . . .

BE HAPPY
WHEN OTHERS
SUCCEED!

IN A **WORLD** WHERE YOU CAN **BE** **ANYTHING** . . .

be open to the idea that you may be the problem!

IN A **WORLD** WHERE YOU CAN **BE** **ANYTHING . . .**

be willing to
make sacrifices!

In a world where
YOU CAN
be anything . . .

BE CONTENT!

IN A **WORLD**
WHERE
YOU CAN
BE
ANYTHING . . .

be the-best-
version-of-yourself!

ABOUT THE AUTHOR

Matthew Kelly has emerged as one of the great thought leaders of our time. His enormous success as an author, speaker, and business consultant is the result of his comprehensive worldview which springs forth from the single idea that we are each here to become the-very-best-version-of-ourselves.

This worldview elevates every aspect of life, from relationships to health and well-being, and from work to personal finances, and beyond. In fact, there is no aspect of the human experience that is beyond the reach of this single idea.

Victor Hugo wrote, "There is nothing more powerful than an idea whose time has come." We respectfully disagree. There is nothing more powerful than an idea that touches everyone, everywhere, all the time. For such an idea, its time never stops coming.

Kelly developed "the-best-version-of-yourself" concept in his twenties, trademarked it, and has been sharing it in every arena of life for more than twenty-five years. It is quoted by presidents and celebrities, athletes and their coaches, business leaders and innovators, though perhaps it is never more powerfully quoted than when a mother or father asks a child, "Will that help you become the-best-version-of-yourself?"

Matthew Kelly has dedicated his life to helping people and organizations become the-best-version-of-themselves! Born in Sydney, Australia, he began speaking and writing in his late teens while he was attending business school. Since that time, millions of people have attended his presentations in more than fifty countries.

Today Kelly is one of the bestselling authors of our times. His books have been published in more than twenty-five languages, have appeared on the *New York Times*, *Wall Street Journal*, and *USA Today* bestseller lists, and have sold more than forty million copies.

He is the founder of Floyd Consulting, a corporate consulting firm that specializes in transforming corporate cultures and increasing employee engagement. Floyd serves businesses of all sizes with its coaching, training, consulting, and keynote speaking services.

Frustrated with traditional publishing early in his career as a writer, Kelly started his own publish company to publish his books and license them to other publishers around the world. He has had incredible success distributing books through non-traditional publishing channels and is widely considered one of the most significant innovators in this industry that has been struggling to find its way. At present, the majority of his books are published under the Blue Sparrow imprint.

Since he was a teenager, Matthew has been a serial entrepreneur. His latest venture is as a partner in a very unique online watch store called *Every Watch Has a Story*. His personal interests include golf, live music, reading, spirituality, investing, travel, philanthropy and spending time with his family and friends.